Reading Essentials® in Social Studies

COUNTRY CONNECTIONS II

CHINA

JOANNE MATTERN

Perfection Learning®

Editorial Director: Susan C. Thies

Editor: Mary L. Bush

Design Director: Randy Messer

Cover Design: Michael A. Aspengren

Inside Design: Michelle J. Glass, Mark Hagenberg

IMAGE CREDITS:
© CHINA PHOTO/Reuters/Corbis: p. 35; © Cristie's Images/CORBIS: p. 37 (right); Stockfood: pp. 31, 33

Clipart.com: pp. 6 (top), 7 (bottom), 15 (top), 18, 22; Corel: pp. 7 (top), 8, 10, 12 (top), 14 (bottom), 15 (bottom), 16, 21, 24 (bottom), 26, 28, 29, 30, 38; Eyewire: p. 14 (top); Map Resources: p. 4; Perfection Learning: p. 34; Photos.com: cover, pp. 2–3, 5, 6 (bottom), 11, 12 (center, bottom), 13, 17, 19, 20, 23, 24 (top), 25, 27, 32, 37 (left), 39, 40, 41, 42, 45; Stephanie Meggers: p. 9

TABLE OF CONTENTS

Just the FACTS!

Location China is located in Asia. Because it is such a large country, China is bordered by many other countries. The largest of these bordering countries are Russia to the north and India to the southwest. The Yellow Sea, East China Sea, and South China Sea border China along its eastern coast.

Mount Everest

Area 3,696,100 square miles

Geographical Features China's large size makes room for a variety of land regions. Mountains, deserts, and coastal regions cover the continent. China also has several major rivers. The Yangtze and Yellow Rivers are two of these important waterways.

Highest Elevation Mount Everest (29,028 feet above sea level)

Lowest Elevation Turpan Pendi (505 feet below sea level)

Climate The **climate** in China is as varied as its land. Cold, snowy mountains on the western side of the country meet a more temperate, or mild, climate in central China. The eastern coast along the Pacific Ocean experiences warm **tropical** weather.

HOW LOW CAN YOU GO?

In China, the lowest place you can go is Turpan Pendi, also known as the Turpan or Turfan Depression. This area of low-lying land is located on the eastern side of the Tian Shan Mountains in China.

Tiananmen Square, also known as the Gate of Heavenly Peace, is a historical area of Beijing that honors the country's Communist ideals.

Capital City Beijing

Largest Cities Shanghai, Beijing, Tianjin, Wuhan, Shenyang, Guangzhou

Population 1,286,975,000 (2003)

Official Language Mandarin Chinese

Main Religion Most Chinese are atheists who do not believe in God and do not belong to an organized religion. **Buddhism** is the largest formal religion practiced in the country.

Buddhist monk

WHAT DID YOU SAY?

More people speak Mandarin Chinese than any other language in the world.

Government China is a **Communist** country. The Communist Party is the only political party with any power in the nation. The country is ruled by a **premier**. The premier is appointed by the president of the National People's Congress. China is divided into 33 government, or administrative, units.

ALSO KNOWN AS . . .

The official name of the country is the People's Republic of China.

Industries mining, machinery, textiles, footwear, toys, food processing, electronics

Natural Resources iron ore, coal, petroleum, natural gas, mercury, tin, tungsten, antimony, rice, wheat, cotton, tea, sorghum, fish

Currency basic unit is the yuan (you AHN)

PENNIES FOR THE PEOPLE

Chinese money is called *Renminbi*, which means "people's currency (money)." The basic unit of Renminbi is the yuan. One U.S. dollar (one hundred pennies) is worth about eight Chinese yuans.

FLYING HIGH FOR CHINA

The red background on China's flag stands for revolution, or change. The large yellow star represents the Communist Party. The four smaller stars are for the people of China. The star arrangement is meant to show the unity of Communist China.

CHAPTER 1

Beneath Your Feet

China's Land and Climate

China covers 3,696,100 square miles. It is approximately the size of the United States. This large area means that there are great differences in the land and climate across the country.

GEOGRAPHICAL FEATURES

Western China has many mountains. The Altai Mountains, Kunlun Mountains, and Himalayan Mountains are three major ranges that run along the western edge of the country. Mount Everest is part of the Himalayas and is the tallest mountain in the world. The western region of Tibet is covered by a huge **plateau** surrounded by many tall mountains. It is known as the "Roof of the World."

Northern China is also called Mongolia. Mongolia is an area of grasslands and deserts. The largest deserts in China are the Takla Makan Desert in northwestern China and the Gobi Desert in Mongolia. Few creatures can survive in these harsh, dry areas.

An oasis in the Takla Makan Desert

The Tsinling Mountains rise in central China. They form a barrier between the dusty sand and soil from the north and the moist winds from the south. Because of this, areas above the mountains are dry plains used for growing wheat and areas below are warm, wet fields where rice is grown.

The Huang He River, also known as the Yellow River, flows from west to east across northern China. This river is 2697 miles long. It gets its name from the yellow soil it carries. The Huang He makes the land around it very **fertile** and good for farming. Heavy rainstorms in the summer often cause the river to flood.

Yellow River

China's longest river is the Yangtze, or Chang Jiang. This river is 3915 miles long. The Yangtze flows south from Tibet. Then it turns east and empties into the Pacific Ocean at the city of Shanghai. Many fields along the Yangtze are constantly flooded, which creates natural rice **paddies**.

LOESS IS MORE

The yellow soil carried by the Huang He River is called *loess* (pronounced "less" or "luhs"). China has large hills of loess soil, many of which provide excellent farmland. The country has the largest and deepest **deposit** of loess in the world.

The land south of the Yangtze River is covered with green hills and mountains. Areas near rivers provide fertile soil for crops. The rest of the land is so hilly that it cannot be farmed.

May to October is the rainy season in the coastal province of Yunnan in southern China.

THE CLIMATE

From the top of Mount Everest to the shores of the Pacific Ocean, the temperatures and **precipitation** in China differ greatly. Snowfall occurs only in the northern portion of the country. Northern China has bitterly cold winters, where the temperature can drop well below zero. But in the summer, this same region can reach temperatures of more than 100°F. The deserts in this area receive very little precipitation year-round.

Southern China is warmer and wetter than the rest of the country. More than 40 inches of rain fall in many southern parts of China. Some cities along the coast have a tropical climate all year long. Cities farther inland experience mild winters.

Seasonal storms called *monsoons* blow through China. In the winter, they carry cold, dry air across the country toward the ocean. In the summer, they return with warm, moist air. The summer monsoons bring rain that is needed for farming but often cause flooding that kills many people and destroys property.

CHAPTER 2

Living Wonders

The Plants and Animals of China

China is home to many different plants and animals. From forests to deserts, there are many different **habitats** in China. Each habitat is home to a unique group of plants and animals.

PLANTS

More than 30,000 plants are **native** to China. This is one-eighth of all the plant species in the world. Many of these plants are used for foods, spices, and medicines. Rice, soybeans, tea, cucumbers, and apricots are food sources first grown in China. Spices from the country include ginger and anise.

Approximately 5000 Chinese plants are used for medicines. Ginseng and gingko biloba are two common Chinese plants that are used to treat mild health problems and increase overall wellness.

Hundreds of years ago, much of China was covered by forest. But today, most of China's forests have been cleared to make room for farms, homes, and businesses. Remote mountain areas are the only places where thick forests still grow. Oaks, maples, larches, and birches thrive in these forests.

Bamboo

A BOUQUET FROM CHINA

Many of the decorative flowers used worldwide were originally grown in China. Rhododendrons, gardenias, jasmines, and primroses are all native Chinese plants.

Southern China has a tropical climate. Rain forest plants thrive here. Evergreen trees and palm trees grow tall. Bamboos, gingkos, laurels, and magnolias are other tropical plants commonly found in China.

Rhododendrons

Western China has a drier climate than other parts of the country. It is too dry for most trees to grow. Instead, several different kinds of grasses and shrubs cover the land.

Magnolias

ANIMALS

China is home to a large number of animals. Unfortunately, many of these animals are endangered. They are often killed for food or for use in medicines. In addition, these animals are threatened when their habitats are destroyed to make way for homes and farms. In recent years, steps have been taken to help some of these animals make a comeback.

Take a look at a few of the interesting creatures of China.

Giant Panda Pandas are large animals with black and white fur. They are about 6 feet long and weigh between 250 and 300 pounds. Because they are so big, adult pandas have few natural enemies. However, baby pandas are small. They are often attacked by leopards, foxes, and other carnivores (meat eaters).

Pandas spend up to 16 hours a day eating! The only thing they eat is bamboo. One panda can eat about 600 bamboo stems a day. A giant panda's body has several special features to help it eat bamboo. Five-clawed front paws with an extra bone that works like a thumb enable a panda to grab bamboo shoots. Sharp front teeth and flat back teeth help the panda bite and chew bamboo stalks. The animal's throat and stomach have tough linings to protect them from bamboo splinters.

> **PEACEFUL PANDAS**
>
> The Chinese consider the panda a symbol of peace.

Their limited diet has led to the starvation of many pandas. Today there are less than 1000 pandas in the wild. The Chinese are very protective of the remaining pandas. Anyone caught hunting one faces extreme punishment—sometimes even death!

Red Panda Red pandas don't look like giant pandas. Their coloring is different, they have long ringed tails, and they are much smaller. A red panda is only about 2 feet long and weighs just 6 to 11 pounds.

Red pandas have long, sharp claws to help them climb quickly and easily through the trees. These animals eat bamboo, but they also eat some fruits and grasses too.

Siberian Tiger Siberian tigers are the largest members of the cat family. They measure more than 8 feet long and weigh up to 660 pounds.

Siberian tigers eat large prey, such as deer, cattle, or pigs. They also eat frogs and turtles. Tigers hunt by creeping through the

> **THE "BEAR" FACTS**
>
> Although many people refer to the cute, cuddly panda as a "panda bear," these animals are *not* bears. They are actually in an animal class all their own!

grass slowly and quietly. When they are a few feet away from their prey, they rush forward and grab it by the neck. The tiger's bite is so powerful that it crushes the prey's throat. The prey cannot breathe, so it dies quickly.

The Siberian tigers in China live in the evergreen forests of Manchuria. They are an endangered species. Only several hundred of these beautiful orange and black tigers are living today.

> **WHERE IS MANCHURIA?**
>
> Manchuria is also known as Northeast China or the Northeast. It is an area that includes the **provinces** of Jilin, Heilongjiang, and Liaoning.

Bactrian Camel Most bactrian camels live in China. They differ from other camels because they have two humps instead of one. The camel stores fat in the humps on its back to provide energy when food and water aren't available.

A camel can also drink 50 gallons of water in a day. After filling up, the camel can go a long time until its next drink.

Many bactrian camels have been domesticated, or tamed. They live in villages and towns in China. Others still live wild in the Gobi Desert.

Bactrian camels have adapted to the extreme temperatures of the desert. In winter, they grow long, shaggy coats to keep them warm. In the summer, most of this heavy fur falls out.

Yak Yaks are the largest mountain animals. They can measure up to 6½ feet tall at the shoulders and be almost 10 feet long. They can also weigh more than a ton (2000 pounds). These huge animals survive on an all-plant diet.

The yak can live in extremely cold temperatures. Its long, shaggy outer coat of fur almost touches the ground. Under this coat is a layer of short, thick fur. All this fur keeps the yak warm and dry.

Extra red blood cells help yaks' bodies absorb oxygen. This is important in the thin mountain air where yaks live. In spite of this, only a few hundred wild yaks remain in the Himalayas today.

People use yaks to carry heavy loads over high mountains. They also drink yaks' milk and use it to make cheese and soap.

Water Buffalo Water buffalo are found in the wetter areas of China, especially near rice paddies. Many farmers use these animals to pull plows, wagons, and other farm equipment. Water buffalo are among the largest breeds of cattle in the world. They can weigh 1500 to 2600 pounds. Their horns can be as long as 6 feet across.

Water buffalo spend most of their time rolling around in mud and water. This helps them keep cool. It also helps get rid of annoying insects, such as flies and mosquitoes, that bite the buffalo's skin.

Chinese River Dolphin Most dolphins live in the ocean. The Chinese river dolphin, however, lives in freshwater rivers.

Chinese river dolphins have very poor eyesight. Instead, they "see" objects by sending out a high-pitched sound. When an echo bounces back, they can locate the object. This is called *echolocation*.

Chinese river dolphins have more than 100 teeth. These teeth are sharp and pointed for catching fish. The dolphins also eat shrimp they find in the river mud.

Chinese Alligator Chinese alligators are shy reptiles that live near the lower Yangtze River. Because much of their natural marsh habitats have been cleared for farmland, these animals are quickly disappearing.

Like many reptiles, Chinese alligators **hibernate** during the winter. They find a warm cave to sleep through the cold, dry months. In the spring, the alligators wake up and look for mates to start a family.

Chinese alligators have a varied diet. Their favorite foods include small fish, clams, snails, rats, and insects.

ON THE MOST ENDANGERED LIST

The Chinese alligator is the most endangered crocodilian in the world. This group includes all alligators and crocodiles.

Golden Pheasant China is home to many different birds. One of the prettiest is the golden pheasant. This 3-foot-long bird has a ring of colorful feathers around its neck. When the male is trying to attract a female, he spreads these golden feathers over his head like a fan.

Golden pheasants nest on the ground in the forests and mountains of central China. Females sit on the nest to keep the eggs warm. Unlike

most other birds, golden pheasant chicks can feed themselves as soon as they hatch. They can also fly by the time they are a week old.

Golden pheasants are a popular captive bird in China. They can be found in parks, zoos, aviaries, and homes around the country.

CHAPTER 3

Looking Back China's History

Chinese civilization is one of the oldest on Earth. Early life can be traced back 400,000–500,000 years. The earliest recorded Chinese history is almost 4000 years old.

THE CRADLE OF CHINESE CIVILIZATION

The Yellow River is sometimes referred to as the "cradle of China's civilization." Scientists believe that China's first people settled in this area thousands of years ago because the land was good for farming and raising livestock. These people became known as the Lungshan.

EMPERORS AND DYNASTIES

Over the years, many different **dynasties** ruled China. Each dynasty was led by a ruler called an *emperor*. Fossil evidence has shown the existence of the Xia (SHEE ah) Dynasty in the 21st–16th centuries B.C. The first dynasty to leave written records was the Shang Dynasty.

Bronze wine vessel from the Shang Dynasty

The Shang ruled from 1766 B.C. to 1123 B.C., when they were conquered by the Zhou (joh). The Zhou ruled China for 200 years. Then wars broke out and divided China into smaller states. Each state had its own ruler.

In 221 B.C., an emperor named Qin Shihuang conquered all of the states in China and established the Qin (chin) Dynasty. Qin Shihuang reunited the nation and formed a central government. He also created standard systems of written language, weights and measures, and money. Qin Shihuang valued education. He set up a system of tests so that only the smartest people could get jobs in his government.

THE GREAT WALL OF CHINA

One of Qin Shihuang's most lasting accomplishments is the Great Wall of China. The Great Wall is located in northern China. It is 4160 miles long, 20 feet wide, and 26 feet high. It is the largest human-made object on Earth.

Qin Shihuang did not have all of the Great Wall built. Before he became emperor, many kingdoms in China were surrounded by walls for protection. When Qin Shihuang became emperor, he decided to join all of these small walls into one huge wall. Millions of Chinese men used clay, stone, sand, and even tree branches to build the Great Wall.

Over the years, many parts of the Great Wall have fallen down or been destroyed. During the Ming Dynasty (1368–1644), some of the wall was rebuilt with stones. Today, tourists can visit parts of the Great Wall, climb its ancient stone steps, and walk through the guard towers.

After the Qin Dynasty, China was ruled by many different emperors and dynasties. Some of these dynasties lasted for hundreds of years. Others lasted only 30 or 40 years. While these dynasties made China a strong economic and cultural country within itself, the country had little contact with the rest of the world.

NATIONALIST CHINA

The last dynasty to rule China was the Qing (ching) Dynasty. This dynasty began in 1644 and lasted until 1911. During this time, China opened some of its western cities to trade with Europe. But many problems occurred between the Chinese and the British. This led to a war and other problems for the Qing Dynasty. Finally, after Great Britain, France, and Russia took control of parts of China, the Qing Dynasty fell in 1911.

At this time, many Chinese people supported **nationalism**. They wanted to have more control over their own country and were angry that European countries had so much influence in China. After the Qing Dynasty ended, a man named Sun Yat-sen founded the Republic of China. He became China's first president and is considered the first ruler of modern China.

THE PEOPLE'S REPUBLIC OF CHINA

The Republic of China lasted until 1949. During that time, many citizens joined the Communist Party. Fighting between the Nationalists and the Communists tore the country apart. Finally, in 1949, the Communists took control of China. In October of that year, the Communist leader, Mao Zedong, founded the People's Republic of China.

Mao Zedong brought many changes to China. He tried to change the country's **economy** so that China could compete with other countries. Zedong's plan was successful at first, but overworked laborers, a lack of funds, and outdated technology soon caused serious problems.

Mao Zedong also wanted to get rid of old customs and traditions in China. He started a program called the Cultural Revolution. All citizens were expected to follow the strict teachings of communism in all aspects of life. Education about past Chinese **culture** was forbidden. Books were burned, and many temples and other historical buildings were destroyed. Those who did not cooperate were put in jail or sent to the countryside to work on farms.

After Zedong's death in 1976, Deng Xiaoping became the new leader of China. Deng Xiaoping put an end to the Cultural Revolution. He established trade and political relationships with world powers. He allowed Chinese citizens to have more contact with the rest of the world. For the first time, people from other countries were allowed to travel freely throughout China. Deng Xiaoping died in 1997, but China has continued to modernize and develop into a country with a strong economy.

NOTES ON COMMUNISM

Communism is a political system where all wealth, property, and businesses are controlled by the government. Ideally all people in a communist society should be equal with the same amount of money and property. However, in reality, a communist government often gives most of the wealth to only a few people and the rest of the population works hard under poor conditions for very little money. In China, the system of communism is often referred to as Maoism.

This portrait of Mao Zedong hangs in Tiananmen Square in Beijing.

CHINA TODAY

China is divided into 33 areas for the purpose of governing the country. There are 22 provinces, 5 **autonomous regions**, 4 **municipalities**, and 2 special administrative regions (SARs). The provinces are Anhui, Fujian, Gansu, Guangdong, Guizhou, Hainan, Hebei, Heilongjiang, Henan, Hubei, Hunan, Jiangsu, Jiangxi, Jilin, Liaoning, Qinghai, Shaanxi, Shandong, Shanxi, Sichuan, Yunnan, and Zhejiang. Guangxi, Inner Mongolia, Ningxia, Tibet, and Xinjiang are the five autonomous regions. The four municipalities are Beijing, Chongging, Shanghai, and Tianjin.

Hong Kong and Macao are two special areas in China. These two regions have their own form of government. They support a **capitalist** economy, where the property and businesses are owned by the people. Because they are still part of China, the country established a "one country, two systems" policy. This means that Hong Kong and Macao can keep their capitalist form of government but still remain part of China as SARs.

Hong Kong

A QUESTION OF BELONGING

China claims that it actually has 23 provinces. It includes the island of Taiwan as its twenty-third province. Taiwan, however, considers itself an independent country. The issue began in 1949 when Communists took over mainland China. Millions of Nationalists fled to Taiwan and set up their own form of government there. Whether China and Taiwan will someday reunite is still a question to be answered.

CHAPTER 4

Digging In to China's

Resources and Industries

MINERALS

China is rich in mineral resources. The country is a leading producer of antimony and tungsten. China also has large amounts of tin, lead, copper, mercury, and aluminum. Iron mining is a major industry in the country.

Large deposits of coal can be found in China's eastern provinces. Coal is still used to run machines and heat homes and businesses in China. However, the discovery of oil and natural gas deposits in the country has decreased the amount of coal used to produce energy.

MEET THE MINERALS

Antimony is a silvery gray metal that breaks easily. One use of antimony is in flame-retardant materials, such as those found in children's clothing and toys.

Tungsten is a hard, shiny, gray metal that is used in lightbulbs and cutting tools.

WATER

China has several major rivers. However, only about five percent of China's energy is currently provided by water power. Several large dams provide this hydroelectric power as well as control flooding on China's rivers. The Three Gorges Dam is now under construction on the Yangtze River. When completed, this dam will be the world's largest dam and hydroelectric power station.

Fishing is an important industry in China. Large fishing boats travel the waters of the South China Sea, the East China Sea, and the Pacific Ocean. A variety of fish, shrimp, scallops, and clams are found in these waters. In addition to ocean fishing, many people fish along China's rivers and **deltas**.

China even has thousands of fish farms. Carp is a common food in the Chinese diet. These fish are raised in special ponds on fish farms.

Fish drying at Cheung Chau Island, a fishing village in Hong Kong

24

Rice paddy

AGRICULTURE

More than half of China's people make their living through farming. This is an amazing fact considering that only 10 to 15 percent of China's land is suitable for farming. Despite the shortage of fertile land, the farm products grown or raised in the country provide enough food to feed most of the nation's huge population.

The majority of China's crops are grown along the eastern coast. Northeastern China produces most of the country's wheat, corn, and soybeans. Rice, potatoes, and tea are grown in the warmer, wetter climate of the southeast. Sugarcane, sweet potatoes, peanuts, and cotton are other Chinese crops.

Pigs and chickens are the most common farm animals in China. Cattle and dairy farmers have to make the most of the little productive grazing land in the country. Today, China **exports** large quantities of meat, eggs, and milk.

MORE THAN A BOWLFUL

Rice is a major food crop in China. These white fluffy grains are the **staple** of the Chinese diet. About one-third of the rice in the world is grown in China.

A worker runs a loom at a textile factory in Shanghai.

INDUSTRIES

Since the end of the Cultural Revolution, China has made tremendous progress in catching up with modern technology. The country is now a leading producer of electronic equipment and machinery. Computers, software, televisions, and other **telecommunication systems** have become major industries as well. The production of farm machinery, automobiles, and other large machines has increased greatly. China has also established a space travel program.

CHAPTER 5

The Many Faces of China

Discovering China's People

With almost 1.3 billion people, China has the largest population of any country in the world. Almost all of its people are of Asian **descent**. More than 90 percent of the population are Han. The rest belong to one of more than 50 other **ethnic** groups, such as the Mongolians, Tibetans, and Manchus.

LIFE IN THE CITIES

Most of China's cities are in the eastern part of the country. Although only about 30 percent of the Chinese live in cities, these **urban** areas are very crowded. Sidewalks are filled with people rushing to and from work or home to their friends and families.

Because it is very expensive to own a car, many people use bicycles to get around. It is not unusual to see a huge group of cyclists riding down the highway along with cars, motorcycles, trucks, and buses.

Most families in the city live in apartments or small houses. Houses are often built around small outdoor areas called *courtyards*. Several families share one courtyard. In some places, families also share bathrooms and kitchens.

Chinese cities usually have many parks. Because their homes are small and crowded, the Chinese spend a lot of time outdoors. They exercise, play games, fly kites, picnic, and visit with friends.

Most adults who live in cities work in offices, factories, or stores. Many work six days a week—Monday through Saturday.

Children start school when they are six years old. They go to school six days a week. Schooling in China consists of six years of primary school, three years of junior middle school, and three years of senior middle school. Education is important to the Chinese. They realize that their people must be educated in order to compete in the modern technological world.

LIFE IN THE COUNTRY

Most of China's people live in **rural** towns, villages, or farming communities. Houses in the country are often made of sun-dried bricks. Like those in the city, rural houses are small and have few rooms.

Rural villages have no stores or other businesses. The villagers must travel many miles to shop.

In China, all members of a family work on the farm. Children work alongside their parents and other relatives to plant and harvest crops and take care of animals. Many rural families still use animals instead of machines to help them farm. For example, oxen and water buffalo are often used to pull plows. Most modern machinery is too expensive for the average Chinese farmer.

Rural children do go to school. However, these children often take time off to help their parents on the farm during busy seasons. Some rural children have to walk many miles to get to the nearest school.

A VERY CROWDED CHINA

China is a very crowded country. Its resources have been stretched to the limit for many years.

The Chinese government has taken steps to control population growth. Chinese couples are encouraged not to marry until they are older and to have only one child. In 1982, the government passed a law that said each family could only have one child. Those who ignored the one-child policy could be fined or lose their jobs. Many Chinese were upset with the law as family is an important aspect of traditional Chinese culture. Recently, the government has relaxed the one-child policy, but it is still a part of modern Chinese life.

Billboard promoting the one-child policy

ANOTHER FACE IN THE CROWD

When you look into the cute, furry faces of the dogs around you, can you tell which ones came from China? Some popular dog breeds that originally came from China include Pekingese, shih-tzu, chow chow, Lhasa apso, shar-pei, pug, Chinese crested, and löwchen.

Pekingese dogs were considered sacred in ancient China.

CHAPTER 6

A Slice of Life

Chinese Culture

FOOD

Traditional Chinese foods vary by region. Rice is the most common food in China—especially in the coastal provinces. There it is eaten at almost every meal. Meat, vegetables, spices, and sauces are often added to rice to create many different dishes. Rice is not grown in the drier north, but fields of wheat there provide flour for noodles.

The western and central mountain regions, especially the Sichuan province, are known for their hot, spicy foods. Seafood is popular in cities along the coast. In southeastern China, people eat small filled dumplings called *dim sum*. Egg rolls, wontons, and potstickers are appetizers enjoyed in southern China.

Unlike people in North America and Europe, the Chinese don't eat cakes, candies, pies, and other desserts very often. Dessert is usually an orange or some other fresh fruit.

Egg rolls

Stir-fry dishes usually include meat (beef, chicken, or pork), vegetables, and a combination of oils, sauces, and spices.

The Chinese use special tools to cook and eat their food. Chinese food is often cooked in a wok. A wok is a bowl-shaped pan with high sides. A little bit of oil is placed in the bottom, and the food is stirred quickly as it cooks fast at a high temperature. This type of cooking is called *stir-frying*.

Traditional Chinese dining doesn't involve knives and forks. Instead, two thin sticks called *chopsticks* are used to pick up food.

CAN I HAVE A BIG MAC AND FRIES, PLEASE?

Today, many **Western** foods are available in China. Hamburgers, fried chicken, sandwiches, and ice cream are becoming more popular, especially in urban areas. Restaurant chains such as McDonald's and Kentucky Fried Chicken are expanding throughout the country.

CHINESE NOODLES

In China, people often eat noodles on their birthday. The noodles are not cut because the Chinese believe that long noodles are a symbol of long life. Below is a Chinese recipe for noodles with peanut sauce.

ingredients

2 tablespoons smooth peanut butter

¼ cup hot water

3 tablespoons soy sauce

1 teaspoon honey

4 cups of lo mein noodles, cooked and drained (Ask an adult to help you cook the noodles.)

½ cup chopped peanuts

directions

1. In a large bowl, mix the peanut butter with the hot water until the mixture is creamy.
2. Add the soy sauce and honey. Stir until well mixed.
3. Add the cooked noodles to the bowl. Stir until the sauce covers all of the noodles.
4. Refrigerate the noodles until you're ready to eat them.
5. Top with the chopped peanuts before serving.

LANGUAGE

The majority of people in China speak Mandarin Chinese. Mandarin is a language based on symbols, not letters. Students in China don't have spelling bees because words are represented by pictures instead of groups of letters. There are over 60,000 characters, or symbols, in the Chinese language.

橘子　　苹果　　香蕉

Orange　　　　Apple　　　　Banana

SPORTS AND GAMES

Although the Chinese spend many hours at school or work, they still enjoy sports and other leisure activities in their free time. Many factories and businesses allow workers to take exercise breaks during the day. These workplaces often have basketball or badminton courts for employees to use.

Ping-Pong, basketball, volleyball, and martial arts are popular sports in China. Swimming and diving are favorite summer activities. In the cold northern cities, many people enjoy ice skating.

Many Chinese play board games. One of the most popular games in China is called *Go*. Players place black or white discs on a board. Each player tries to surround the discs of the other player with his or her own discs. There are so many possible moves in *Go* that the game has been called the most complicated board game in the world.

Go

Another Chinese game is *mah-jongg*. Players collect painted tiles and try to get winning combinations. You can often see people playing *mah-jongg* in parks and outside restaurants.

HOLIDAYS

Several major celebrations take place in China throughout the year. The Chinese Lunar New Year falls in January or February. This holiday is a family time with special meals, dances, parades, and firecrackers. Children are often given gifts of money in small red envelopes. The color red is a sign of luck and wealth.

INSTRUCTIONS FOR A HAPPY CHINESE NEW YEAR

- Pay off all debts before the new year begins.
- Do not sweep on New Year's Day so the good luck is not swept away with the dirt.
- Be careful not to break any dishes or use sharp knives or scissors, since harm will bring bad luck for the coming year.
- Wash your hair before the holiday to avoid money problems in the new year.
- Do not eat white foods such as tofu and fresh bean curd because the color white is unlucky and means death.

The Festival of Lanterns is held at the end of the Chinese New Year. The Chinese eat sweet dumplings to symbolize unity. They hang colorful lanterns to guide guests and spirits to the celebration.

Dragon dance performed during the Festival of Lanterns

Another important holiday is the Mid-Autumn Festival. On this day, Chinese people make wishes on the full moon. They also eat special pastries called *mooncakes*. Mooncakes are round (like a full moon) and filled with a sweet paste, fruit, or jam.

In addition to the national holidays and festivals, each ethnic group in China has its own celebrations. The Mongolians gather for the Nadam Fair of the Mongol every summer. The Dai hold a Water-Splashing Festival where they have prayer ceremonies, dust Buddhist statues, and sprinkle water on one another for well-being. The Lisu people climb poles with sharp knives sticking out of them during their traditional Knife-Pole Festival. A Tibetan bathing festival in late summer is said to bring good health for the rest of the year.

A CHINESE CALENDAR

January 1	New Year's Day
January/February	Lunar New Year
March 1	International Working Women's Day
April 5	Qing Ming or Pure Brightness Day (in remembrance of the dead)
May 1	Workers' Day
May/June	Dragon Boat Festival
June 1	International Children's Day
August 1	Army Day (honors the People's Liberation Army)
September/October	Mid-Autumn Festival
September 10	Teachers' Day
October 1	National Day (celebrates Mao Zedong's founding of the People's Republic of China)

THE ARTS

China has a long tradition of art and literature. Chinese artists often include symbols of nature and the seasons in their work. Mythical animals, such as the dragon and the phoenix, are also popular designs.

During the Ming Dynasty, the Chinese made beautiful blue and white clay vases. They were admired around the world and became known as "china." Today, vases, dishes, and other decorative art are made out of china.

The Chinese have their own style of painting. Paintings are often done on silk or on thin paper made of bamboo. Most Chinese paintings are done in black with very little color. The shape and thickness of the brush strokes are as important as the picture itself. Many Chinese artists combine **calligraphy** with their painting.

China's literary tradition dates back thousands of years. Ancient Chinese writers created poetry, folktales, and other stories. Some of these were about mythical creatures. Others were about everyday people and events. Two of the most popular ancient Chinese writers were Du Fu and Li Po. Confucius was a Chinese philosopher and scholar whose writings and teachings were highly valued in traditional Chinese culture.

Birds and Flowers
by Pan Gongshou

Confucius

37

Chinese opera performer

Storytelling is an important tradition in China. Storytellers can still be found in parks today. They tell traditional and modern stories to audiences of all ages.

Music is also an important part of Chinese life. Chinese music uses a different scale than Western music. The Chinese scale has only five tones instead of eight. Many children learn to play musical instruments at a young age. Two of the most popular instruments are a stringed instrument called a *qin* and a recorder called a *xiao*. Chinese people also enjoy the opera. Chinese operas tell traditional stories and feature music with acrobatics.

THE MONKEY KING

The Monkey King is one of the most popular figures in Chinese legends and operas. In these stories, the Monkey King belongs to a Buddhist monk. The two travel around the world and have many adventures. The Monkey King sometimes causes trouble, but he always protects his master from danger.

To learn more about the history of the Monkey King and to read an illustrated story of his adventures, visit this Web site.

http://www.china-on-site.com/monkey.php

CHAPTER 7

What's Ahead?

A Look at China's Future

China has changed rapidly in just the past 20 years. The country faces even more changes in the 21st century.

A CHANGING COUNTRY

The Chinese economy has changed dramatically since Deng Xiaoping came to power. New technologies have created business opportunities and strong economic growth. Yet many of China's people still live in poverty with few modern conveniences. As China's economy prospers, the country needs to spread the wealth and benefits among all its people.

China's huge population continues to threaten the well-being of all citizens. Resources and space are stretched thinner and thinner. Plans that combine the needs of the country with the traditions and wishes of the people must be developed and carried out.

Finding ways to balance the needs of its people with the demands of the rest of the world continues to be important to China. Although contact with Europe and the United States has helped China in many ways, it has also compromised the country's traditional way of life. In addition, the Communist government sometimes creates conflict with democratic, capitalist countries. If China is to become a solid world leader, it must blend its beliefs with those of other world powers.

The Chinese also struggle to keep the country unified. Some groups, such as the Tibetans in the west, the Uighurs in the northwest, and the Taiwanese to the east, want independence from China. The Chinese government does not agree. Finding a compromise is essential to keeping peace in the country.

FREEDOM OF CHOICE

Unlike in the United States, Chinese citizens don't enjoy many personal rights and freedoms. Freedom of speech, freedom of religion, and freedom of choice are very limited in China. People are not allowed to speak out against the government. They are also not allowed to belong to certain religions or other groups that might threaten the government. They must follow government regulations about where they can live, when they can get married, how many children they can have, where they can work, and where they can travel. People who disobey these rules face severe consequences.

Although the Chinese people today have much more freedom than they did in the past, they still lack many of the basic human rights that citizens of other countries take for granted. Many other countries in the world have criticized China for the way it treats its people. As China has more contact with Western nations, it may have to change its official policies. In the future, this may lead to more conflict between the government and the Chinese people, as well as between China and other countries.

THE ENVIRONMENT

China has many environmental issues. Industries in the cities have poisoned the air and water. Pollution has also caused acid rain, which kills plants and destroys habitats. Farmers in rural areas use pesticides and other chemicals that pollute the soil and groundwater.

Trying to feed a huge population with a small area of fertile farmland has also caused damage to the environment. Overuse of land for growing crops and grazing animals has led to **erosion** and **desertification**. This has reduced the amount of productive farmland even further.

The country also uses tremendous amounts of water and other natural resources, such as coal and natural gas, to run its industries and meet the needs of its people. These resources are nonrenewable. There is a danger that some of them may run out in the future. China must control its water usage and pollution and find other ways of providing energy for homes and businesses.

China is working to solve its environmental problems. It recently formed the Natural Environmental Protection Agency. This organization has started a tree-planting program to save farmland in northern China. Planting trees helps prevent soil erosion. The government has also passed new laws to limit industrial pollution.

LOOKING FORWARD

China is one of the most mysterious and complicated countries on Earth. For thousands of years, its people have overcome social issues and created a beautiful culture that is a blend of the past and the present. China will continue to integrate the challenges of the future into its rich heritage.

INTERNET CONNECTIONS AND RELATED READING FOR CHINA

Just the Facts!

http://www.gigglepotz.com/china.htm
This kids' site includes Chinese crafts, puzzles, and zodiac calendar fun. Explore the links for more information on Chinese culture.

http://www.enchantedlearning.com/asia/china
Pick up some general information on China, and complete a variety of fun activities, such as filling in maps, learning Chinese numbers, and designing a Chinese flag.

Chapter 1

http://www.china.org.cn/english/shuzi-en/en-shuzi/gq/htm/dilitezheng.htm
Travel through China with this overview of the major plateaus, basins, plains, mountains, rivers, lakes, and other land features in the country.

Chapter 2

http://flora.huh.harvard.edu/china/mss/plants.htm
Find out more about the importance of China's plants with this site and its links.

http://chinatown-online.co.uk/pages/travel/wildlife.html
Discover the wildlife of China—its primates, cats, pandas, alligators, and other animals.

http://www.nationalgeographic.com/kids/creature_feature/0011/
Check out the featured animal at this National Geographic "Creature Feature" site and learn more about the amazing panda. Click on other featured animals, such as the tiger, for more information as well.

Chapter 3

http://www.china.org.cn/e-china/index.htm
Click on "history" to get briefed on China's history from ancient times to modern days. This "China in Brief" site includes a timeline of the country's dynasties.

http://www.enchantedlearning.com/subjects/greatwall/Allabout.html
Tour the Great Wall of China through these facts, map, and links.

http://www.time.com/time/time100/leaders/profile/mao.html
Learn why Mao Zedong made *Time* magazine's list of the most important people of the 20th century.

http://www.chinatoday.com/city/a.htm
Travel through the provinces, regions, and municipalities of China with this map and overview of the country's political divisions.

Chapter 4

http://www.china.org.cn/e-china/index.htm
Click on "agriculture," "industry," or "tourism" to explore these areas of the Chinese economy.

http://www.pbs.org/itvs/greatwall/
Follow the story of the Yangtze River and the Three Gorges dam project and its effects on the environment.

Chapter 5

http://library.thinkquest.org/26469/cityscape
Tour 12 major cities to learn more about urban life in China.

Chapter 6

http://www.globalgourmet.com/destinations/china/
Get a taste of China with this introduction to Chinese cooking for everyday meals and special occasions. Try some of the recipes provided.

http://www.tuvy.com/chinese/learn/learn_mandarin.htm
Learn the basics of Mandarin Chinese, and impress your friends and family with these Chinese greetings, numbers, places, and foods.

http://www.travelchinaguide.com/intro/festival/index.htm
Celebrate China's national, ethnic, and tourism holidays and festivals with this online overview.

http://www.kidsdomain.com/holiday/chineseny.html
This fun site for kids includes information, crafts, puzzles, and other activities associated with the Chinese Lunar New Year. You can also check out Chinese calendars, nursery rhymes, and folk and fairy tales.

Chapter 7

http://www.chinatoday.com
Find out what's new in China today with this overview of the country.

http://www.china.org.cn/english/index.htm
This news Web site features current event stories, as well as information on China's art, culture, government, laws, sports, and much more.

∘ ∘ ∘ ∘ ∘ ∘ ∘ ∘ ∘ ∘ ∘ ∘ ∘ ∘

Ancient China by Arthur Cotterell. An Eyewitness book on ancient China. Dorling Kindersley, 1994. [RL 6.8 IL 5–9] (5863106 HB)

China: The Culture by Bobbie Kalman. A celebration of the cultural achievements of China's 4000-year-old civilization. The origins of many of China's celebrations are traced back to the country's ancient past. Crabtree Publishing, 1989. [RL 4.5 IL 3–9] (4172001 PB 4172001 CC)

China: The Land by Bobbie Kalman. Examines China's ancient and recent histories in a simplified but meaningful way while presenting information about China's development and modernization. Crabtree Publishing, 1989. [RL 4.5 IL 3–9] (4171801 PB 4171801 CC)

China: The People by Bobbie Kalman. Candid photographs, intimately portraying the Chinese people going about their daily business, depict how the changing face of China has altered the daily lives of its people. Crabtree Publishing, 1989. [RL 4.5 IL 3–9] (4171901 PB 4171901 CC)

Dropping In On China by David C. King. A title in the Dropping In On series. Rourke Book Company, Inc., 1995. [RL 5.7 IL 3–8] (5877506 HB)

The Great Wall of China by Leonard Everett. The story behind the building of the Great Wall of China. Simon and Schuster, 1995. [RL 4.2 IL 1–5] (5927501 PB 5927502 CC)

The Great Wall of China: The Story of Thousands of Miles of Earth and Stone by Elizabeth Mann. A title in the Wonders of the World series. Fire Fly, 1997. [RL 4 IL 4–6] (5780306 HB)

Search for Gold Mountain: Coming to America from China—1850 by M. J. Cosson. Li Ming and his father are lured to America after hearing about the wealth to be found in California. Perfection Learning Corporation, 2001. [RL 4.7 IL 4–6] (3171901 PB 3171902 CC)

Tales of China retold by Janice Kuharski. The magical world of Chinese legends and fairy tales is brought to life. Perfection Learning Corporation, 1998. [RL 3.4 IL 4–9] (5524401 PB 5524402 CC)

RL = Reading Level
IL = Interest Level
Perfection Learning's catalog numbers are included for your ordering convenience. PB indicates paperback. CC indicates Cover Craft. HB indicates hardback.

Sundown at a cove in Guilin, China

GLOSSARY

autonomous region   (aw TAH nuh muhs REE juhn) area in China that has some local self-government

Buddhism   (BOO diz uhm) religion based on the idea that spiritual goals are reached by giving up worldly possessions and desires

calligraphy   (kuh LIG gruh fee) art of painting written symbols or characters

capitalist   (KAP uh tuh list) type of economic system based on the private ownership of business and property

climate   (KLEYE mit) usual weather in a place

Communist   (KAH myou nist) type of political system in which the government controls the economy, wealth, and property (see separate entry for *economy*)

culture   (KUHL cher) beliefs, customs, and social activities of a country or group of people

delta   (DEL tuh) fertile land near the mouth of a river where the river empties into an ocean (see separate entry for *fertile*)

deposit   (dee PAH zit) amount or quantity of a material found in one spot

descent   (di SENT) coming from a particular place; heritage

desertification   (diz er tuh fuh KAY shuhn) process by which fertile land becomes desert land due to overuse or climate changes (see separate entry for *fertile*)

dynasty   (DEYE nuh stee) series of rulers who belong to the same family

economy   (ee KON uh mee) country's system of making, buying, and selling goods and services

erosion   (uh ROH zhuhn) wearing away and movement of soil by wind, water, or ice

ethnic   (ETH nik) relating to a group that shares a common culture (see separate entry for *culture*)

export   (EKS port) to send to other countries for sale

fertile	(FER tuhl) good for growing crops
habitat	(HAB i tat) place where a plant or animal lives
hibernate	(HEYE ber nayt) to go into a sleeplike state in the winter
municipality	(myou nin suh PAL i tee) city that has the same status as a province (see separate entry for *province*)
nationalism	(NASH uh nuh liz uhm) loyalty and devotion to a nation or country that often results in a desire for political independence
native	(NAY tiv) originally growing or living in an area
paddy	(PAD ee) field covered with shallow water where rice is grown
plateau	(plat OH) flat raised area of land
precipitation	(pruh sip uh TAY shuhn) moisture that falls from the sky in the form of rain, hail, snow, sleet, etc.
premier	(pruh MEER) head of a government
province	(PRAH vins) region or division of a country for government purposes
rural	(ROOR uhl) having to do with life in the country
staple	(STAY puhl) main food in the diet of a group of people
telecommunication system	(tel uh kuh myou nuh KAY shuhn SIS tuhm) technology for communicating across distances, such as satellites, telephones, fiber optics, etc.
tropical	(TRAH pik uhl) having a warm, wet climate (see separate entry for *climate*)
urban	(ER bin) having to do with life in the city
Western	(WES tern) relating to countries in the Western Hemisphere, most commonly European countries or the United States

INDEX